What's That Noise?

Original story written by Jade Michaels

Illustrated by John Bennett and John Dunne

One day, Violet Flowers
goes to live in an old, blue
house on a hill.

This house is
perfect for me.

Violet Flowers is nine
years old. She's got a small
suitcase and a new violin.

A family of mice live in the old, blue house too. Merlin and Mina live downstairs in the dining room. The door of their mouse house is next to the fireplace.

Every morning at eight o'clock, Merlin and Mina go to look for food for their breakfast. They carry the food on a skateboard.

Mmm. I like apples, bananas and grapes, Merlin.

Phew! I'm tired!

One day, Merlin and Mina hear
a terrible noise.

They run out of their mouse
house. They are very scared.

Then they go to find Uncle Matthew. Uncle Matthew is a very clever mouse. He lives in the kitchen in the old, blue house.

What's that noise?

I don't know. Come on, Mina. Let's find Uncle Matthew!

Uncle Matthew lives on a shelf
next to a window.

There's a terrible noise
in the dining room.
We're scared!

Uncle Matthew is very worried.

Oh, dear! What is it? Let's investigate!

Uncle Matthew goes with
Merlin and Mina. He hears
the terrible noise.

Be careful, Uncle!
The stairs are
very high!

Uncle Matthew
is very brave!

Listen!
The noise is coming
from upstairs.

Then Uncle Matthew goes upstairs.

Violet Flowers is in her bedroom. She is playing her new violin. She can't play very well. The noise is horrible!

Uncle Matthew speaks to Violet.

Hello, I'm Uncle Matthew. What's your name?

Violet Flowers is very scared of mice.

She screams and drops her violin.

She jumps on a table.

13

Uncle Matthew comes
downstairs and tells
Merlin and Mina
about his adventure.

Oh, good!
No more noise!

14

Now Violet is scared and her violin is broken.

Now our mouse house is quiet again.

Goodnight, Mina.

Goodnight, Merlin.

Violet Flowers is so scared she
runs away and she never goes
to the old, blue house again.

Activities

1 Look at Mina's family. Write the names.

pandarg   margand
grandpa   _____

add   umm   neluc   iuntae
_____ _____   _____ _____

throbre   steris   anim   sounic
_____ _____ _Mina_   _____

2 Look at the picture. Write _true_ or _false_.

1 It's two o'clock.   _true_

2 The violin is downstairs.   _____

3 There's a banana in the kitchen.   _____

4 The fireplace is in the bedroom.   _____

5 The skateboard is in the dining room. _____

6 There are three tables in the house.   _____

3 Find eight mice in the picture. Write where they are.

| next to   behind   under   on |

1 There's a mouse _behind the door_____ .

2 There's a mouse _____ .

3 There's a mouse _____ .

4 There's a mouse _____ .

5 There's a mouse _____ .

6 There's _____ .

7 _____ .

8 _____ .

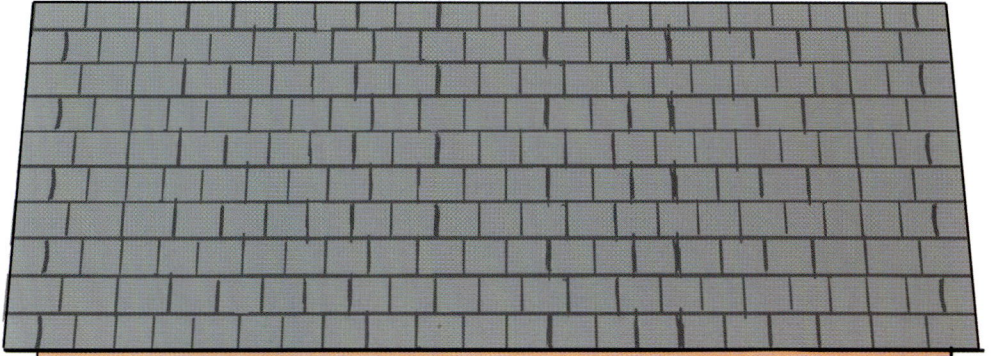

4 Write the numbers. Find the secret number.

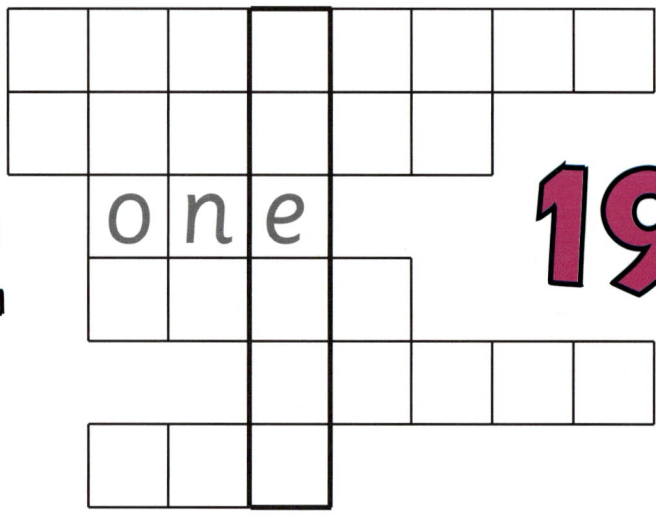

8 **5** **12** **19** **1** **10**

one

The secret number is _____ .

5 Write the times.

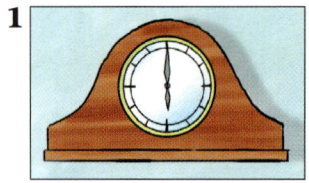
It's six o'clock.

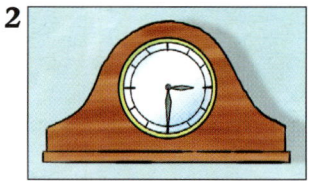
It's half past three.

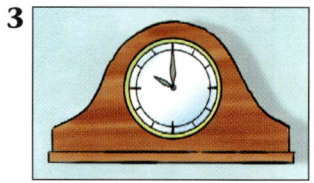
_____

_____

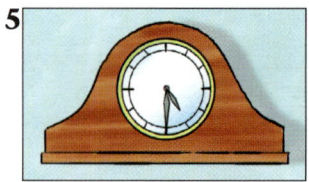
_____

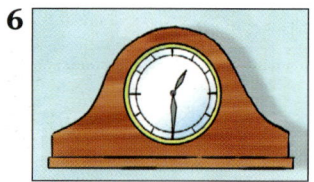
_____

6 Complete the story.

screams	jumps	runs	sees	~~hears~~	drops

1

It's breakfast time. Merlin ____ *hears* ____ a noise.

2

He _____ a cat.

3

He _____ the banana.

4

He _____ .

5

He _____ off the table.

6

He _____ into the mouse house.

Picture Dictionary

hill

suitcase

violin

upstairs

downstairs

kitchen

dining room

bedroom

eight o'clock

shelf

window

stairs

table

door

fireplace

mouse

mice

hear

   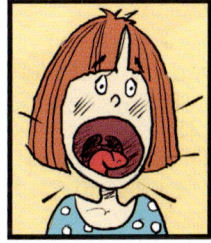

| drop | jump | carry | scream |

| brave | tired | scared | worried |

| breakfast | food | apple | banana | grapes |

| high | broken | noise | skateboard | quiet |

Macmillan Education
Between Towns Road, Oxford OX4 3PP
A division of Macmillan Publishers Limited
Companies and representatives throughout the world

ISBN 1 4050 2507 7
ISBN 1 4050 5719 X (International Edition)

First published 2002 Macmillan Education Australia Pty Ltd
This edition © Macmillan Publishers Limited 2004

Illustrated by John Bennett and John Dunne.

Printed and bound in Spain by Mateu Cromo

2008 2007   2006 2005 2004
10 9 8 7 6 5 4 3 2 1